Infinite Variations

Marci Nelligan

Copyright 2012 by Marci Nelligan

Black Radish Press
www.blackradishbooks.org

First printing 2012 in the United States of America

All rights reserved. No part of this book may be reproduced without the publisher's written permission, except for brief quotations in reviews.

Acknowledgments
The author would like to acknowledge the following people for their contribution to this work, or to the sanity of the writer, a relative term to be sure, but sanity enough to finish it, finally.
To my daughters and Lee for the ever-evolving wonder of the world we make. To my family, for everything, from my cellular makeup to that college education. To Bret and Laura for their constant, enduring intelligence and humor, their big hearts, their rare brand of friendship. To Nikki and Steve, the family I'm not officially related to, which nurtured, and loved me better than most. To my pals in Lancaster, and in the F&M English Department, who have helped make this place in every sense my home. To my spiritual family, Matt & Tama, Ken & Lauren, Kabi & Steven, and my fellow commune members Jen & Brent, and Kasey & Michael, for their general otherworldliness and stellar good fun. To Nick and Nicole for big-time inspiration and solidarity. To Marthe Reed and Cara Benson for their keen, insightful editing of this book. To all the Black Radishes for making such a fertile, gorgeous garden. And to Nicole Mauro, a dear friend, a huge inspiration, and one serious kick in the pants, a huge thanks for bringing this collective to life.

Thanks also to the editors of the following journals for publishing some of this work.
Pages 1, 2, 5: *eratio*
Pages 3, 6: *The Tiny*
Pages 7–8 : *Word For/Word*
Pages 1–3, 5–11: *Dusie limited edition chapbbook*; reprinted in *Jacket*
Pages 11, 20–22, 35–36, 39, 43, 48, 50–51: *New Orleans Review*
Page 31: *Foursquare*
Page 32, forthcoming *The Denver Quarterly*

LCCN: 2011963722
ISBN: 978-0-9825731-8-1

Infinite Variations

Poems composed of randomly selected text from the
Origin of the Species *and the* Hebrew Bible.

We cannot explain the world
—various causes
construct for god
bodies in one country
whilst in another
trees or bread.

The hand will strike
segments of a limb used solely
for locomotion
its enemies will change to orchids—

through the occasional *here*
a mamma-blood apparatus
secretes nutritious fluid.

Mankind acquired reason
this should be this
and also *that*

closer and—all the more
a perfect mind.

Near the head
exists a close analogy—
the tail.

Before the eyes
plumes of birds,
teeth of certain lizards—

under my thigh
your hand
in electric intervals
finally lost
its transition.

Spoken in the ears
as well as the cave,
trees that were buried
now mature

—the same country
put a field of organs
in manifest irritation.

The land is old
and powerful
in defense of which
is something new.

Let (A) be common
and my hand would seek it.
Stolen by day or stolen by night

I brought you
sleep eluded
from my eyes
(represented by the outer dotted lines).

You see that it is mine

(thus) in your house I
was torn-by-beasts—
unequal distances
for twenty years.

I would make good the loss
as we saw in the second chapter

my letters
now accompany
their parent diagram.

To improve she became
pregnant & bore three varieties.
Many days passed
in equal steadiness

—a son bore a name,
—a son caused him to die.

To sum up,
she adapted the seed
to preserve the mountains,
which kept one
on the ground.

What I mean
may illustrate this case.

We wander much
in lesser numbers.
We die with
what we've made.

What would you give me
for four hundred years' servitude—
count the stars, can you count them
connecting together
proceeding from north to south,
lowland to upland &c?

Your reward goes out
from your own body,
raised only to the rank of doubtful species.

In a parallel story
vultures descend, intercrossing
"the species." There was deep
 slumber-fright and great
darkness falling.

The sun changed
its intervals.
Many outlying islands
around a continent.
Structures. Very small steps.

The children,
unconscious,
knew "affliction" had come.

Today, your nervous filaments
reflect an account of me—
at every step
a multitude.
I have served you large bodies of facts,
I found in your eye
an optic nerve.

Your words are seven subdivisions—
slight and gradual rays
removing from each
specked articulata
this destitute lens.

Muscular movements
do something
perfect as converge—

a modified curvature
known as "we,"
simultaneous and therefore
true.

Where the manufactory fell afoul with special parts or organs it was the cupbearer and baker actively at work. After these events the king's secondary sexual process became infuriated. They were closely regulated in the dungeon house, imprisoned and fixed. In being useless, they came to differ. Then the two of them dreamt a dream, each his own in a single night. The chief baker specialized in a particular function—he could not overcome his tendency. The cupbearer arose saying, "A vine was in front of me, an extraordinary size branched off from a common parent, higher and higher but I could not climb it!" The guard came in the morning and saw they were dejected. "Here," he said, "your faces are average, not extraordinary, but I understand. They're correlated by specific views. You will be standing higher in the second chapter, actively at work, each rudimentary scale adjusted to his dream, each man his own interpretation."

I have no power
an aberration of light across the domain of sensations.

Who am I, or if not *it?*
Nature has taken it all: "you" is plural
here: as opposed to "upon."

A lapse of time between the external
and internal world tends
to make incongruities of reason—
even the most perfect
may err as myriads have.

One might say legitimacy is not
in order. Extinct even.

Indeed, this is the sign I sent:
The image on the retina will be modified.

Nothing is a difficult foundation,
contradicts the syntax "this that I am."
As for the optical machine,
it sends me to you

a delight of rapid instances
each part
by each part.

I am inclined to suspect
we never see
what is important—

a kingdom divided
among insects branching
the main nerves according to
philosophical difference.

Facts are perplexing—
hardly two agree,
each after its own tongue
protean or polymorphic.
The saying is "at the beginning."

O dimorphism,
two sexes
connected by difference
also show
one point—

Earth in larval state;
the great central ganglion
of changing expectation.

Women advanced in days become more powerful, acted upon by special difficulties. Where is their pleasure? Why does she laugh? Within herself any ordinary muscle is hurried through and finally lost, a little electricity when an animal is irritated. He stood over her and said, "Conceive a wondrous character finely enveloped in know-how and trivia—a real homologue of the electric battery!" She made bread cakes and ran to fetch a theory, saying "Shall I really give birth to a young ox now that I am old? Is anything surprising, so little known of anyone?" At a set time, she returned to his tent, tender and fine, serving his nerves in a manner reserved for prey. She said, "I am changing character, my plumes worn with distribution. I give my milk to fertile females while time revives my impotence. Only here is behind us—this ceases to be."

Lament if you will
sterility across a land
whose excess pays our ills—
death is the first difference
and all are gone who had become.

From before to always
what differs
is the man who rules,
so fertile death holds
our names in his mouth,
a bramble of arrangement.

Why act
when there's the limited
good of a little pleasure?
A system caved in, buried
by resemblance.

Our hands are heavy
and explain in causing
the things we once believed.

Individuals are born
speaking of the elements,
the word, no doubt
a so-called "animosity."

Whoever objected to that deal?
Organisms dug one another
but to chemists speaking
of the elective affinities, he called
you and your seed *remembering*.

Gravity made space
as a "you come to me" condition
so he spread his tent there, natural
in the sense of 'natural selection.'

Owing to slaughter-site,
& nature of the well, he
made them a drinking fest, just
as we moved on from there.

Why survive?
So we may bear fruit
and also
quarrel over it.

To be collected in futurity.
To last an age.
A distant epoch of gold in the mouth—
a house destroyed by history.

Shallow seas endure
their animals,
preserve our bodies in
incessant formulation.

A bed of light
accumulating
for good or ill
the naked remains
of our extinction—

a city of words
a language of duration.

He dreamt
the horse—
a tendency of fact
changing form.

From where do you come
if not this nakedness
if not a single ancient character
carrying the future
on hobbled legs?

Inheritance bears its marks—
sometimes an honest man
pretends, and even the true
are no more pure.

A horse, a horse.

What is probable prevails.

A graduated series
of light proves its presence
—such are its qualities,
such is a subject
seen but not discussed.

Your face, alive
of order, a circle
that comes through
the domestic variation
of descendant theory.

We are brought into life
anticipated on the same
division, instruments
that briefly play.

So wholly, so slightly
insufficient, we believe
as we endeavor
this continual instinct
for being, or to be.

Either leave the nest or enter
—the month is constantly July.
House-people are in the house
carrying their slaves in their jaws.

On the other hand, it may be June
—morning and evening close
like doors, and one day belongs
to nothing except the bread
in your hands.

Then the year is twenty-nine
yards distant—another country
leaving its masters to
our bodies.

Come, lie beside me like a road—
let your heart do the unusual work
of escaping your eyes
while our habits migrate
overland.

Having left everything,
this haunting variation
offers no great spectacle,
like the dead without their garments
at one time thought to be
both present and alive.

We admire the scent by which
males make a thousand useless
drones as independent
acts, for the power
of stinging is useful.

Once we take the orchid,
we comply with poison,
progenitors of
ingenious purpose.

But if you circumcise desire
existence becomes difficult
—the perfect elaboration of chance.

All the same, we give you our daughters
and your daughters we take—
a useful exchange of social goods.

Love or hatred,
it's all the same.
We settle our difference
in land rich with pollen,
slaughter our young
to destroy reproach.

Unity, those poor men thought
—a house believes its eyes.

This domesticated world has parts
—you can tell the oil from the flax.
Yet our origin is a wilderness
crossed out and absurd.

The cattle breed skeletons,
a nation humped and mingled,
our wild blood tamed
of its habits.

In artifact, in instinct
reason holds an inheritance
of dust and flint.
One man builds a city
while another names its dogs.

Hardly anyone has established
his veins without the poppy
flows, its descendent need.

Less belief than structure,
more tribe than collection,
the present goes on
its long discovery
authoring the past.

Here, open ocean
and nothing remains
but silver water, silver fish.

A body can hide
by conceiving the imaginary,
by breathing its
incipient self
into otherwise.

One might escape
or be devoured—
it's all famine in the land
and drowning in the water.

So we collect our organs
into wing structure,
a stage of chance
supplanted by the probable.

This life excludes all
particulars, spinning immateriality
from one edge of the border
to the other edge.

The skin is diffused by proportional
numbers. Inside, a wilderness
of false remarks.

Perhaps you anticipated posterity—
a future raised in manuscript form—

or grasp at expectation
in reference to your offspring.

The faithful sense
the same comparisons,
make the eye a well
of incipient water,
the hand a kind of covenant.

.

Allusions illustrate our struggle—
life the same
or nearly similar.

Nothing, a fade-out
phenomenon enters the gap
between dream and man's production
—a tint of wishes
grouse-red to catch
the eye and intimate
some period of the slightest
troubled cycle.

As before, the mottled
white of winter half expressed
an ordinary face.
In name god promised
higher workmanship—
a second-generation
figurative, if not destroyed,
in its larger context
understood.

One ovule holds
the flowers of curious
structure, their dimorphic
and trimorphic arrangement
necessary now we know
the mind as an inutility
of instances.

Trifling remarks excite
no special use, the ears
meet as mere morphology
just one time to illustrate
night as orchids present,
or the assumed
difference of ruin.

Even to speak, to turn aside
when one imagines it
upsets the significance—

people stand for something
human, a tactile prayer
seeking its direction.

In his hand he took the fire and the knife
without obvious cause.

There are many points of similarity.
Nourished in a mother's womb
the young are eminently sensitive,
weak and dwarfed within the eggs.

I am my son, he said.
Ironic. The throat slit
of silk moths and willow
leaves, as with the embryo
some hint of sacrifice.

Unsuitable ideas offer up
an answer—the original act
as imperfection—the lamb,
the torch, the brand.

He said, "We wish to bow down.
We wish to build a happy
ending, even if our young
must perish of belief."

From the beginning,
the world was a colored map,
its labor and its wars a lapse
of reason, a submarine surface
between *occurred* and *felt*.

So did their lives spread
out with burden
and with sediment
as continents extend
beyond our will—

a neighborhood of
enemies to tear and append
a remnant of the same
formation

each age a partial state of things
each upheaval in service to the next

Every crawling thing
depends on the apple
or the egg—

not to devour but to hold

everything doubled
in a ruined world
as a thousand suffer
and so survive.

All rapidly, all sense
this breadth and height
a physical doctrine
in number growing
closer to the animal.

To seed the length of years,
to force the inevitable
& follow together
whole into whole.

Allow me to kiss between
insect and insect
setting your face toward its lies.

A parasite on the prey
most foolishly
checks his watch—

such humble joy
to number their wits
while cats & mice speak
of captive frequencies.

All season or year
the American forests grow
on ruin, caught up in a dream
of false night while war
feeds its hands into habit.

A problem of action/reaction
—all-striving, all-knowing.
Bodies like feathers
fall—another
potent entanglement,

but how false the dependency—
our beautiful view—
on trees we cannot see
for all these trees.

In you or not you remain
as you are
—more beautiful alive,

but how to hold the heart's
membrane in custody?
Something like distress has come
and we did not listen.

Truth was sifted from
your mouth like mud from water
—a test of stiff concern
beginning the day god said
do this and do that,
while our awe traversed
the length of credible reason.

Obliquely we became
something else, obtaining from
our bones an incomparable axis
—the entire middle distance
inward & articulate, like minute
prey saying stay,
and stay.

My mouth, being close, speaks
words, how there are
allied propositions,
how the neck is kissed
to save the truth.

Any part of conviction
sustains the disinherited
—a bat nearly hopeless
less its wings.
Still, we want to stay
alive, by no means sensible.

Some years, doubt harvests
our uselessness
—all plows and reproduction
weighty in the making.

So female, so plainly of
power but rarely,
so rarely
come to it.

Brush the you over
mine if you know how,
before able men spring
forward with foreign influence.

We come near each other
many days and years slowly
just to touch with the same
anthers toward it,

or move out of the conjoined
suddenly toward the pollen
of some other flower.

All the numerous make
out and fertilize, never
pure but habitually possible.

This garden of the goodliest part
is really giving it up—
one and another.
A heavy presence holds
it all together,

the stigma of each
beautiful greeting
mutually exhausting
—an ill-fated blessing
—a farewell that would come.

Night has deepened into shallow basins,
distance uniting its points of intersection
wider and wider as the dislocated eye.

Your name remains a perfectly flat surface
converted by diameter, cylindrical cells
that guide a bird across the river.

This is a problem of appearance and belief,
straight lines scalloped away to nest between ourselves.

Suppose a pyramid wrestled with its architecture
as our excavation broke into several
spheres of influence,
the socket of the thigh, a certain face.

So we are tested by experiment,
each instance uttered as
the edge describes what's left—
that part of truth is will
and all power lies in taking it.

There is nothing holy here-—the relative weight of the body is a saying—an object, an instinct, three new moons the color of bamboo. More than one writer has asked why the mind is confined to its forms, but instead we played the whore and got pregnant and thought of apes. Why why why. The question is intellectual; you can't expect a savage to predict. I sent a message first to make a point—we are completely lost. By the aid of our hind legs, one has risen higher in the scales, the other runs quickly on the ground. Even recognizing that, you can't find among the excrement of birds a single living insect. Oh constant tendency to neutralize, to belong, to grow a body in the body. We hold ourselves motionless. We imitate but we are not. Yes, it is rude, yes it recurs, and no one can solve the simplest problem.

Wings of birds in little clusters
seven & seven & five arise—

another ill-looking appearance
as if wind-formed or fragmentary
—all the same—all falling.

Forget what you believe—
evidence converts the variable
into been, light into its value.

So, too, a dream depends,
 a vast embryology
of facets and formation—
an instance crystallized
as a wing becomes a
word & all thought
interpretation.

Morning extracted
from the hemisphere
of nothing a formation
of night—tertiary, as if
restored—and now
commonly, I admit,
a distinct series.

We change position
like an animal—
I call it the fact
of sessile frequency,
chalked into existence
without stalk or specimen.

There is trouble. There are
instances. We can interpret
a single ear from all this wind
—a stratum where each man
sprung, a house
and all its sayings.

Still, evidence
to this effect insists
we are impossible—
each instance more abrupt
each fact a servant to the dream.

Which capsule of power to believe
one great with seed
or hunted with pincer and with bow?

The links of the chain
arise in deciding whether
you are blessed or damned,

and sometimes
the same island
is its own archipelago.

I bow down to reason
with what common
people call exaggeration.

Whether butterflies arise
or not there is grain and wine
and out of it all we come trembling
to be, to cry, to make a delicacy
of those who damn us.

So it is with human gradation
and the fat earth it furnishes.
One is always the same—
some product of another.

Under an evident atmosphere
birds incline north
—life at greater depths
changing color
(true or not
a lovely action, as a stone
through clear water
tumbles in the light).

But what is the greater hope?
—not the fluctuating sea
—not the domestic opposite we lay ourselves on

Two series organized as animal,
light shaped in the time it takes
to voice a thought or fly.

Who is the same again,
except to say, birds possessed
by climate act or wait
depending on the evidence
as hands, like reason,
lose and hold.

Select a view and all
points flatten, so simple
we can only say
the mouth connects us
to our archetypes.

Inside the body, silver
membranes form a child.

You perceive a pattern, the mouth
says "transpose, transpose"
but there is no signal
no connection.

At the edge of the frame
a hand in ordinary gesture.
Someone is calling you
infinite and it pleases
you, a modification of the clouds.

Once you had purpose
but the similarity lost its
explanation.

Still, each day something ordinary
—a child inside
the body as wings fold
in the framework of the animal
and we exist as hands exist—
part curiosity, part bone.

The need to vary is tenanted between
you and me, but we have lost the power
to escape. Disused, diminished wings incapable
of flap; their flight became this latter agency—
our directions gone, our nature. A man
accumulates, a man survives, so lost
the size and weight of the body drift
like continents, and I, an island broken
off, not relic, my reverence is doubt—the bird
that cannot fly, the surface of these answers
selecting whether anything can be. Only water
and this, our tendency to go on breathing.

The most ingenious stem

could not support them

—light and incoherent, a sort of chamber,

and itself hollowed out into

curious fleshy ridges

a "continual procession" of

lateral wings which went to (another)

and settled in the country of gigantic flowers,

this orchid into which drops of almost pure

water continually fell

and acquired and were carried away.

And viscid, and variously shaped

—a flower conceived in spirit of witness

and its nectar, like a secret

when you stand above

that parts, and waits, and serves.

Change is an atmosphere
immutable as bone
and we, slightly more
than this apparent complexity,
lay as in the weight of water.

Consider inclination
—the way the air holds its organisms,
your hands living as they yield
the limit of our difference.

The depth of this condition
is to utter lovely instances
—not truth, but
a backwards course bitterly conceived.

So simple, so rich
our plastic disbelief.
Follow a sight
and it disappears.
Give the sea a name
and its name produces reason.

Pick a spot we can discern.
In the midst of heaven, death
but not here—here the beautiful
come about like the seldom found
ruin of a whole world.

Many pray to these ashes
—a still place, a perfect supposition,
above all, dusky and mottled
so that each separate rock
gives off an edge.

For instance, consider blue
an image we can specify,
and bear the guilty
like a city its pigeons.
Such ideals sweep denial
like a feather.

Truly, it is strange
—some are pure though their marks
are terminal, the outer and inner
an unknown venture coloring
the air an extraordinary white, or black.

To see it, we must make one thing
of two, belong to
what we lack.

For all its loins and tails,
desire is your nature
its nature your slave.

For a long time the subject was not
'how' or 'when' but
which are you?

Not remarkable, not certain
each word a form of whether.

Sometimes I find myself trembling
and say, true, I am connected
to the way it is, even though this fat
earth makes variety, one is always another.

Hope sexes things up
like butterflies exaggerate their delicacy
and we all come trembling
after reason, as if being
human were enough.

One and one and one
islands and archipelagos
describe the doubtful
and the damned

—the same blessing
—the same belief capsule

A butterfly called
wonderful if only to arise.

Something distinct
rises or falls in
its origin
like a dialect of structure.

We established the language,
grew to love a red mouth.
The first fault was to dwell
weary on the name.

Sometimes I change
the immediate animals
sometimes the best
takes more than usual.

Once I was on notice for
what I wanted,
insensible as fashion—

something just growing
there, seventeen deviations
from perfect, a little distinct
and halfway to dying.

The essence of origin
does not endure.
Out of rash
and afflicting qualities a
self bound to earth
by the philosophy
to remember.

Hearing it all as it went,
the religious feelings of any silent yes
—divine lips of steady
misrepresentation, the attraction
of constraints—

like gravity,
binding and steady,
upholds its own
command "to be something
permanent" or on its own axis—
merely to be.

Natives inhabit temperate zones
and inter-tropical rivers,
but the dominant form
is continental. We, with
weapons and spikes, not ritually
pure, we are everywhere.

So, too, the difficult
affinities as we isolate our accidents
—mountains, islands on the land,
the height of this stage endemic—

this is the sweep of the willing
to curse and kill, a glacial wash
of first extinction.

God loves you for your doubt
and sometimes,
toward the turn of sunset,
he loves you for your evil.

We should respect connecting links
between man and his garment.

We have to believe the 'you' is not afflicted
and the widow, inextricable, not
measured by her years.

A modern, how potent, influence.
Return, yes, return to
all the doings of your hands.

Too much stress fathers sin
—you, broken or interrupted
—you, cut off by many means.

There will always be reason
or if not reason, ignorance.

The grape, the olive
an occasional transport.

And when you die,
may it extend, may it
affect the earth like
an orphan of chaos
lessened by neglect.

Furnished with eyes,
one has a view

—a weaver engraving holiness
in the explanation, a thread of
silence, of pure gold.

To see is to fix,
yet the blind tell
of a seam edge surrounding
the world, opening all around,
twisted but not split—not sight
but the feeling of sight,

as from a cave this protean habit
to write and rewrite
what we are, or what we see.

This ordinary, this secluded flowering
of rain, of seed, of sleep-endured
descent and darkness—

this human amblyopia
preserves our eyes lest they
breech their own severity.

When one sins, breaking faith
we feel almost anything—
what is placed in one's hand
not the same, but sufficient.
We add to it, we care
the mere inflection, the angle of the jaw
and how I have been called
and how it returns to presence
in so many forms
like finding a lost object and denying it.

This the human system—
so our guilt, so our artistry
an insects' wing folded
like a hidden community,
that we might bear our iniquity
or somehow believe.

To be purified one must acquire
habits—a state of body
between instinct and action.

Wonderful animals, what purpose we have
held above the living water declaring
life itself a metaphysical possibility
—*the cedar wood, the scarlet worm, the hyssop*

Our sin is to embrace the flesh,
a gift of whole and utter faculty,
as without knowing why a bird migrates
and lays her eggs, and time impels her premise.

In the open field the bird
is a live bird, the blood its blood
and we wash in the water—
all our wholeness measured
like a grain of wheat, a dose of days
that we offer over and over
as the lamb its innocence,
the now slain bird
its well-worn song.

Now we are floating
—twisted cords
intercrossing.
A man and a woman
on profoundly deep seas.

This mammalian enterprise
occupies the size of things,
a forfeit, a full yield
—of yourself you make the vineyard
of yourself the plow.

Direction is a sign of life—
a man takes a woman and comes in to her
like a garment or a shell,
and perhaps whole countries are
made new, perhaps transported.

How to settle or turn,
bring out of two
what is easily more?

Together, perhaps attached
we home ourselves with struggle
stocked in consequence.

And she thinks of distant islands.

And he spreads his garment out
before the elders of the town.

From a height, people disappear with their particulars until the side of the face and the shoulder become a double of the land like colored drawings of old horses—and maybe we perish in the details, a state of mere collection, rejected for our fear. These are dark and narrow views; I have reason to believe in distant devouring, an improbable approach, but one conquered by survival. The hand is ancient, yet nothing marks the body more plainly than woe, a subject of bleakness that rests in the feeble casing of the world. Let us turn, let us go out to meet what's left—as much written as we are to be.

The heart has placed the will into
servitude and in an instant we are blind
—too much the power of nature,
—too much consumed.

This is the body in ignorance
—the lip, the teeth, the jaw.

To think, to feel
we play with signs
like tongues
play with their meaning.

Understand, the humble
make a structure of the past,
the spontaneity of pain
like rain or hail.

You see a field
and locusts in the field
—the stubborn
thunder of their wings—

and know, before a heavy
heart deny the will,
belief is gone.
So organs play
the frequencies of living.

From year to year, winter
turns white, its glacial absolutes
the scale of our circumstance

—as if by mathematics we are fitted
to our habits, this flesh
a uniform of time so that wherever
we look, a face turns back
but is not a face we know.

Your body, a figure in
scale, will perish in complexity,
over and over as if time
turned back to itself—that face,
white in its utter absence
and, so, not monument but condition—
a thousand years accumulating
its own innate law.

And we, parent to the line,
work as though to embalm
our own uncertainty,
both being here, insistent,
both the ovum and the seed.

In aestivation or absence,
all depends on very little—
the moon on water, night
its insects, the mind
on all it might have lost.

True, you are not
the one who plants
your life, but lame or blind
only dwell on it,
only bear it day by day
like seed.

To pour it out like
blood and observe
the sheer constancy
of choice, as an embryo
affording indications
of its value,
every loss a first, every first
a kind of difference.

We offer of what we are
affinities
to make author of
our illnesses

a hunger sufficient for a herd,
a day, a year, a number.

Endless forms most beautiful
evolve while this planet cycles on
—a ration of increase from the flinty rock,
a wilderness of awe.

As a consequence,
being inspires its reflection,
burning snakes and scorpions, thirsty
soil where there is no water.

Originally, we breathed
capable of future.
Now the gold in our hearts
brings a consequence of less-improved
belief, a famine of conception.

Yet, in our hands and in our houses,
nature brings these senses
into other exaltation,
simplicity being power
like a river increases our direction
and crossing over it, thus crossing.

If I may personify, nature will be called she. The sea will be called he. She is a bone-strong donkey crouched among the fireplaces. He squats like a lion, his eyes darker than wine, teeth whiter than milk. She cares nothing for appearance, nor the staff between his legs. How pleasant is the land, she thinks, the long-backed quadrupeds, those peculiar sheep. He ties his young colt to a crimson tendril; washes his raiment in wine, his mantle in the blood of grapes. She makes a pigeon, then a long-legged foreigner, and finally some food—she is good at this. He does not exercise; therefore his flanks are laboring. He takes up his scepter and upends some boats, then stops to rest. She goes one better, modifying the internal organs of every living creature. Finally he bows down to her, conquered. How perfect, she thinks. Now I possess the thing that would resist me.

Cast from god, we kill ourselves with fury and with frequency.
If nature is a swarm, the swarm must be apportioned.
If the ground chokes with our tendencies, then the anger is our anger,
stocked thickly with our causes, our eggs held in our hands.

How the future seeds the present, thousands of scattered points
marking our dependencies. We take them, ever so little, into hand to
suffer or to increase, our pretty hearts, not what we are, but what we
limit, a vast estate of words uprooted from its fortune.

After Baudelaire

When I view all beings not
as special but disgraceful
—worms crawling through
the damp earth—the world, once broken,
has much light thrown.

A woman clothed in nakedness,
and the man who lies with her,
keeping in his body a lineal
cataclysm so desolate that
eminence becomes infirmity.

I foretell a lapse of distance,
birds tangled in the bushes,
a body satisfied.

We are mere matter, dying—
a common confidence of dirt.
O iniquity, the lapse ennobles—
one must kill the corporeal just to be.

Biography:

Marci Nelligan's publications include chapbooks *Dispatch* (with Nicole Mauro), *Infinite Variations,* and *The Book of Knowledge,* all from Dusie Press. In addition, she was the co-editor of an interdisciplinary book on Jane Jacobs, titled *Intersection,* from Chain Links Press. Her work has appeared in *Jacket,* the *Denver Quarterly, The New Orleans Review, How2,* and other journals. She was the 1999 recipient of  Poets & Writers "Writers on Site" grant and has an MFA from Mills College in poetry. She teaches creative writing at Franklin & Marshall College and lives in Lancaster, Pennsylvania, with her husband and two daughters.